David Hiscock

David Hiscock

zelda cheatle press

4

In the Time of the Bluebells

1987

CONTENTS

Sally
1983

STATES OF THE BODY DAVID ALAN MELLOR

In Baudelaire's prose poem, 'The Double Room' there is a foreshadowing, as if in a tarnished mirror, of David Hiscock's perverse spaces. Baudelaire describes a *"room that is like a reverie. A room that is truly soulful, where the stagnant atmosphere is lightly tinted with rose colour and blue"* [1] . The text gestures towards deep atmospherics and the mysterious indolence of flowers and muslin. This closeted idyll is then punctured by the arrival of the mundane in the shape of a bailiff, or someone from a publisher, wanting copy. Baudelaire calls this figure a Spectre. But with Hiscock the Spectre has always already entered into this narcotised world of the frame's interior and has blighted the flowers and skins of humans and fruit. Besides, in Baudelaire's poem this interior world is already inhabited by a demon – two, perhaps – the "benevolent demon" who has granted him this enchanted interior, and "the Idol", a woman, an object of terrified admiration and desire. This kind of metaphysical world filled with beings in profane ecstasies is related to the claustrophobic, daimon inhabited, settings of Hiscock's photographs of the eighties. For example, around **HEAD WITH LAURELS** 1985 [page 15] there is an ambience of the ritual and ceremonial; the portrait might be that of a sacrificial Temporary King, in the sense of Sir James Fraser's 'The Golden Bough': an incarnate god inspired, in a trance. [2] A peculiar, raked head, overwhelmed by its crown, suffocated by the laurels, an honour turned sinister. It might also be the head of the young prince and rival of Ivan, in Eisenstein's 'Ivan the Terrible', with its occluded signs of the epicene. Here the meanings which could attach to 'Head with Laurels', drift towards the ramifications of camp taste structures. Here is Dante as a distressed mod: a crustacean, a snake or lizard; possessing the languid wasted look of the Charing Cross Road New Romantics of 1981.

The place of ritualism and colour as an enrobing element in Hiscock resembles, in part, their situation in the art of Yves Klein. Like Klein, Hiscock disembodies his figures, dipping them in painterly suspension. Yet it is the autumnal, tonal (English Impressionist) element in Hiscock which sets him aside from Klein's clarity of blue, his primal 'mediterraneanism'. Instead he is spectral, tonal – as if tracking Blake's 'The Ghost of a Flea'. His photographs are populated by spiritual trainees, ephebes, such as the shaven headed acolyte in **UNTITLED** 1982, [page 20] who might be involved in rites, in the kind of performative metaphors and acts around

Dr David Alan Mellor is an independent curator, writer and Senior Lecturer in History of Art at Susex University

1. ed. Michael Hamburger, Charles Baudelaire 'Twenty Prose Poems' 1968, pp.20-I,p.20.
2. cf. The priestesses of Apollo who ate sacred laurel, v. Sir James Fraser The Golden Bough 1993, p. 95.

photography which the decadent Fred Holland Day accomplished in London around 1900. They are robed in a sepia suspension of milk and coffee. They are wrapped in soulful introspection, spiritual inwardness being here signified by postures of sleep, a disciple's rest, which is then scored across by griffes, scratches which double, in crude lines, the features of eyes and lips. Here a certain spiritual-ism of phantom cloud substances is mortified by ash as an element showing loss, in some beautiful petrifying aftermath, such as the world saw in the apocalyptic news photographs of the aftermath of the Mt. St. Helens eruption in 1980. The pale lunar illumination of tragedy was specific to Hiscock in the late 'eighties. There is a Keifer-esque, almost solarised light arising from the rose stems in UNTITLED 1985 [pages 18-19], with their thorns muted against the snow or ash of the olive branches with which they are juxtaposed. This is a light from dusty clouds, or an enervated cocaine dust fall, which powders the formerly living with a new delicacy, the melancholy pleasures of bouquets destined for pompe funebres.

At times Hiscock's photographs look incommensurably archaic. Even before he made the Egyptian series of TRANSMUTATIONS in 1994 [pages 90-91], he had forged photographs which seem to have been taken in antiquity, perhaps in Thebes or in Pompeii. One such is AARON 1987 [page 21]. On a wooden panel with a red ochre and grey surround, blistered and distressed like a miraculously surviving item of furniture from a desert antiquity, is a Nubian head, its neck formalised, extended. It looks out on faraway sands under an oddly clouded sky with a Pharaonic gaze, like the OLYMPIC LONG JUMPERS 1992 [page 40], who resemble Kalahari bushmen stranded in a giant sandpit under a stained sky. Aaron was the patriarch of the Jewish priesthood, a colleague of Moses during the Exodus across dry sands and the Dead Sea, whose priestly rod, transformed into a serpent, was all powerful. And so his head is also transformed into a figure of phallic authority. (And are the palimpsests around his temples reminders of the mistranslated 'horns' of light which played around Moses' head when he returned with the Tablets of the Law? Or are his horns erased to deny some terrible apostasy, an image of a black devil who might elicit our sympathy?) Aaron joins a hideous Judas in TOWARDS ACELDAMA 1989 [page 25] in a range of sanctified or damnable Judeo-Christian dramatis personae in Hiscock's larger narrative of lost powers, initiations, and endurances which diabolically whisper, with the perfumed wood of Sumatra, in Baude-laire's Invitation to the Voyage, "return to me".[3] Here are parchment exposures in the photo-studio of the remote

3. op. cit.

past, one example being **SALLY** 1984 [page 6], who could be a servant of the Queen of Sheba, portrayed in a manner which suggests Irving Penn in the late 1940's, as a shrouded being out of time. These are pictures which have survived abrasions, grit and the toxic floods of the ancient world.

Against the phallic power of Aaron's patriarchal head are the more 'fluid identities' of which Alphonso Lingis has written in Foreign Bodies, the development of liquid economies around the body. In Lingis' suggestion of *"the coding of male fluid as a rare resource…"* [4], there is some approximation to those atmospheric fields of stained, wet, splashed grounds in Hiscock. As Baudelaire had described the stimmung pervading The Double Room, it was as a place where fluid insinuated itself as a ghostly protagonist: *"An infinitesimal odour most exquisitely chosen, which is mingled with a very slight dampness, floats in this atmosphere"*. [5] It is this dampness which spreads across the film and the print in **UNTITLED** 1982 [page 20]. In a more robust key, several of his Olympic Games photographs [page 44 and 46] depict swimmers whose bodies are extended and travestied by water-borne lights, eddies, troughs and shadows. These bodies are simultaneously below and above the water surface, that treacherous plane of chaotic and catastrophic surfaces. Now the body, in Hiscock, has become deliquescent, an undrying film of special effects on the print surface. Once riven into chaotic pools and slivers, Hiscock was opening the way for his representations of the body that might be counted as abstract – with the Transmutation series, where a slow motion camera traces himself making minimal movements so precise it slices the body in jets of time into further ripples and propels it toward a phenomenology of shimmering water.

Hiscock's fictional universe was fabricated as a precious and rarefied zone, however sinister. It was also the site of tricks and special effects, the trucage of wipes and smears and mannerist chiaroscuro. But in his sooty spider's way of handling he occasionally used dripped and haunted techniques related to those most favoured decorative techniques of 'eighties interiors, ragging and marbling. But his mid and late 'eighties pictures are decidedly not the sites of Thatcherite triumphalism in the realm of the visual. In **THE DEATH OF CLASSICISM** 1991 [page 35] he gave a summary lynching to a fluted classical column, that other returned fixture of 'eighties postmodern Neo-Classicism. This is the nearest he came – very sardonically – to the enchanted constructed mythologies of Calum Colvin, his fellow RCA student and studio neighbour throughout the 'eighties until 1991. But

4. Alphonso Lingis Foreign Bodies 1984, p.146.
5. op. cit. p.33.

where Colvin presented a re-enchanted world of consumer debris, memory and myth, Hiscock moved to a distinctly disenchanted view of contemporary culture. From the beginning, the immaculate surfaces of consumption are absent in Hiscock, and the repellent and the abject and the vicious make an accusatory appearance to spoil and soil the pacified Thatcherite pastoral. Later still, shifting from a tenebrous horror – the eccentric English Gothick world – Hiscock became, by 1992, a belated Venetian with the liquefaction of all matter in his scanned photo-finish pictures. With these photographs he pursued that element of decoration and fabulous surface beyond the monochrome of his earlier works and onto the rich marbled revetments of St.Mark's, flickering and uncertain, or the pleated satins and velvets of Fortuny's Delphus robe. The pleats in his photo-finish portraits are folds in time, chasms with passages to those dim auratic associations of the material textures of past histories – chain mail or the threading of tapestries. From the corrupt, muddied, smoky matter that comprised his pictures until 1993, Hiscock passed to the incorruptible, the mineral worlds of his Transmutation series. In these he found true marble, and dragons' teeth like silken spooks among the erratic deposits of his own body, trying to stay still before the scanning camera, transmitting his states of health and being under minute scrutiny and translating them into vivid striations of ruby, amethyst and pearl.

There is a chimerical aspect to Hiscock's representations: they are multi-part fancies which descend upon concocted fetish objects, like **THE GATES OF HELL** 1989-90 [pages 26-27]. Now these monsters, these chimeras, are composites: in this case they are geographically, as well as figuratively, outlandish, since both the tailor's dummy and the legs of the stuffed bird were photographed by Hiscock in Saint Gengoux, near Macon in France. (The bird was found in a painter's chateau which was, according to Hiscock, "Ghormenghast-like" [6]). The gates belong to some 19th century industrial vernacular – massive, spiked, iron-bolted, covered in pitch, which he found propped up and abandoned in the street close to Blackfriars Bridge near his studio in Southwark Street. They are bleak, Dickensian trophies that act as screens upon which mutilated bodies appear, headless and bodiless, carrying the scarifications and cuts of modernisation in front of a frieze of naked combatants fighting in an ashen battlefield of clay waste. This was, Hiscock says, *"a personal version of hell"*. It was not so much Dante-esque, as a vista of brutalisation through banality- the damnation of normalised domesticity entailing

6. David Hiscock, in conversations with the author, November 1994. All subsequent remarks by David Hiscock originate from these conversations.

"wash the car on Sundays" – transformed into an inner landscape of subjective horror. In this he followed Robert Rauschenberg who populated his variant of Dante's Inferno with petrol spirit transfers of basketball players from newsprint photographs at the turn of the 'fifties. From Rauschenberg's Combine paintings, such as 'Trophy III (for Jean Tinguely)' (1961), certain formats and procedures may have been adapted by Hiscock, like the remnant of a ritual veil which is tied between the uprights of a nineteenth century window frame, or the totemic bird, athletes and splashed-out grey clouded scenarios of 'Manuscript' (1963). The latter technique, an expressive sombre erasure, characterised Rauschenberg's art in the early 'sixties. It reappeared in the 'eighties, in the heyday of Neo-Expressionism, as a pictorial device in the work of Anselm Keifer, Ross Bleckner and Joel-Peter Witkin, where it carried a heavy weight of loss. Hiscock shared with them the prospect of funereal scenes with a filmy ground exposed, scratched and seriously fogged into a panorama of decay which became an illustrational hallmark of that decade. These were special effects which connoted a certain kind of anxiety, with promptings and intimations from a tattered past which possessed a threadbare authenticity that was now forfeit in the age of micro-electronic popular capitalism.

Perhaps Hiscock is a gatekeeper, given the repetition of screens and portalled niches and doorways in his art, onto archaic domains of fantastic dramas, of underside visions through flyblown windows of the spirit in dingy weather. In 'The Gates of Hell' he illustrates a drastic version of those dim aching states of being that used to constitute the purgatories of English (and Welsh, especially Welsh) Sundays. He escapes this inferno into artificial paradises in the majority of his pictures, but these remain paradises that can abruptly collapse into flares of misery and pain; exotic places that have turned dark and are Anywhere out of the World, in the title of Baudelaire's prose poem, (itself a citation of Thomas Hood's evocation of visionary negative nocturnes and his poem, 'The Bridge of Sighs'). Later, say by 1993, with the Transmutation series, Hiscock turned from these scenes of staged agonies to less easily retrieved pictures that were not so much romantic scenes as 'abstract' records of endless lengths of interior states, distanced by an improvised photo-finish camera. But the imagery of passages was recovered in his piece **TRANSMUTATION:ROSETTA STONE** 1994 [pages 90-91], where the Rosetta Stone took on a monolithic architectural role as a frame: at the same time it rippled like a curtain and stood as unmoving as the basalt rock from which the Stone was carved.

82
I
91

Head with Laurels

1984-85

Three Backs

1983-85

Untitled

1985

Untitled
1982

Aaron
1987

Three Graces
1988-89

Towards Aceldama
1989

The Gates of Hell
1989-1990

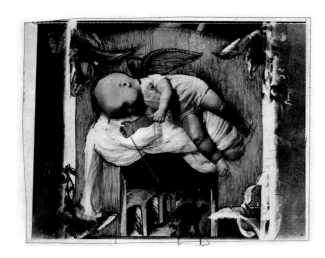

Seven Ages

1989-90

Ombra Mai Fu

1990

The Fire Sermon

1991

The Death of Classicism
1991

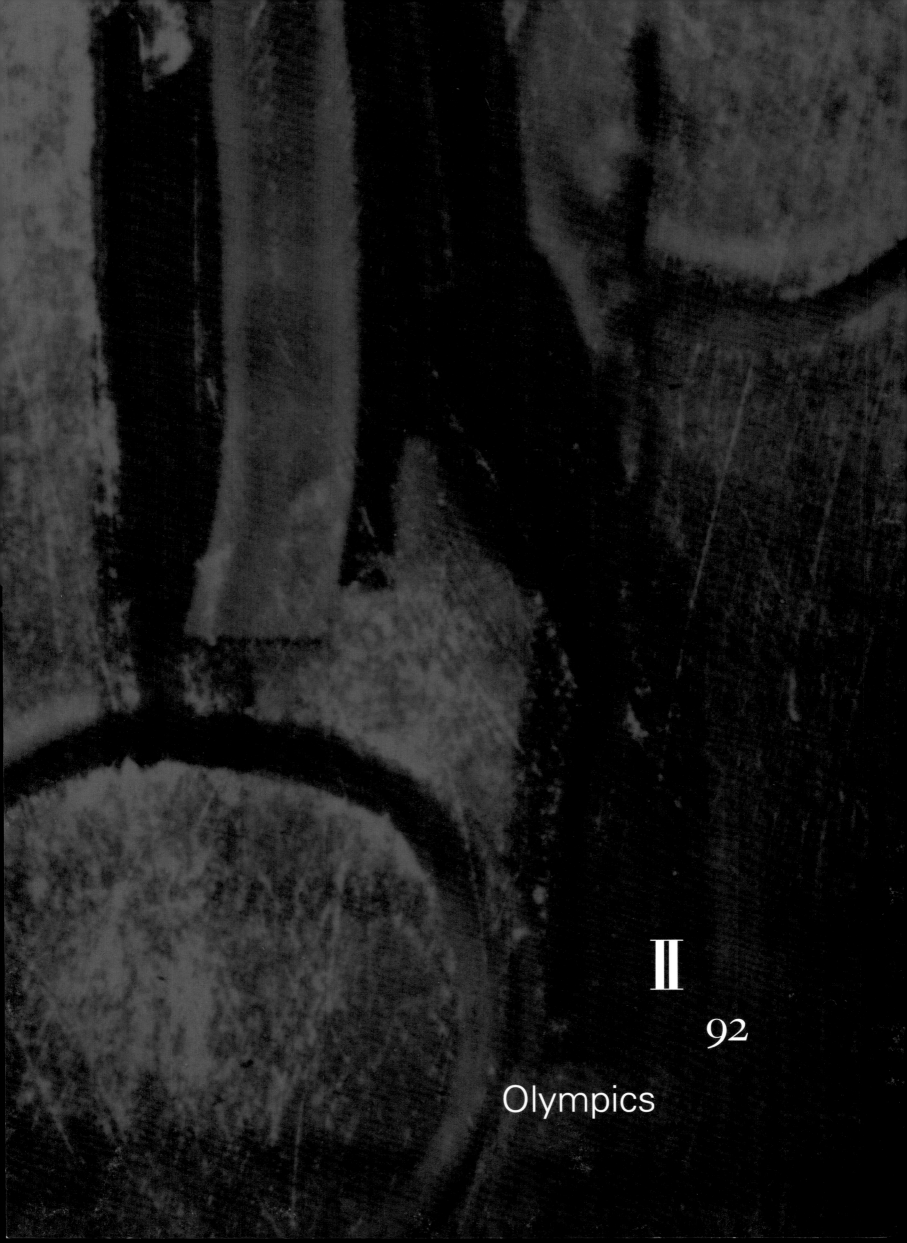

II

92

Olympics

Head with Laurels

1992

Long Jumper

1992

Long Jumpers

1992

Kris Akabussi

1992

Unknown Swimmer

1992

Adrian Moorhouse

1992

Tracey Miles
1992

Two Wrestlers

1992

Duncan Goodhew
1992

Equipment Still-Life Series

1992

Gravitation I & II
1992

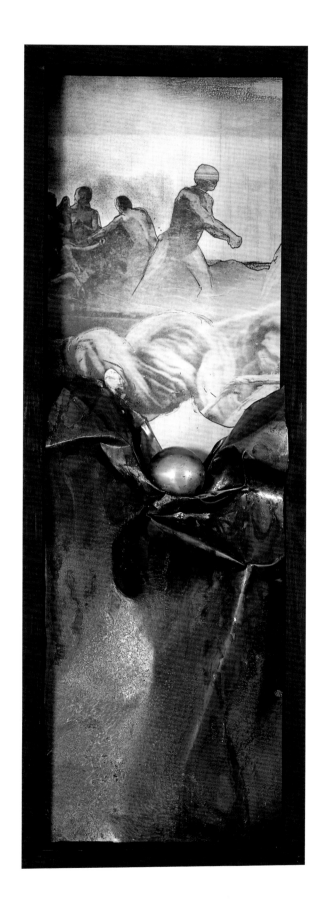

Anamnesis

1992

III

93

Gravures

60

Materia Prima
gravure mono-print
1992-93

Materia Prima
gravure mono-prints

1992–93

Materia Prima
gravure mono-print, maquette
1992-93

Untitled
maquette
1992–93

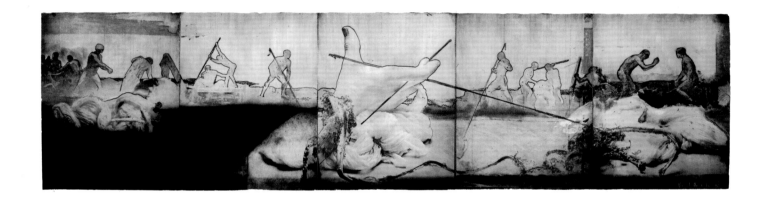

Untitled
gravure mono-prints
1992-93

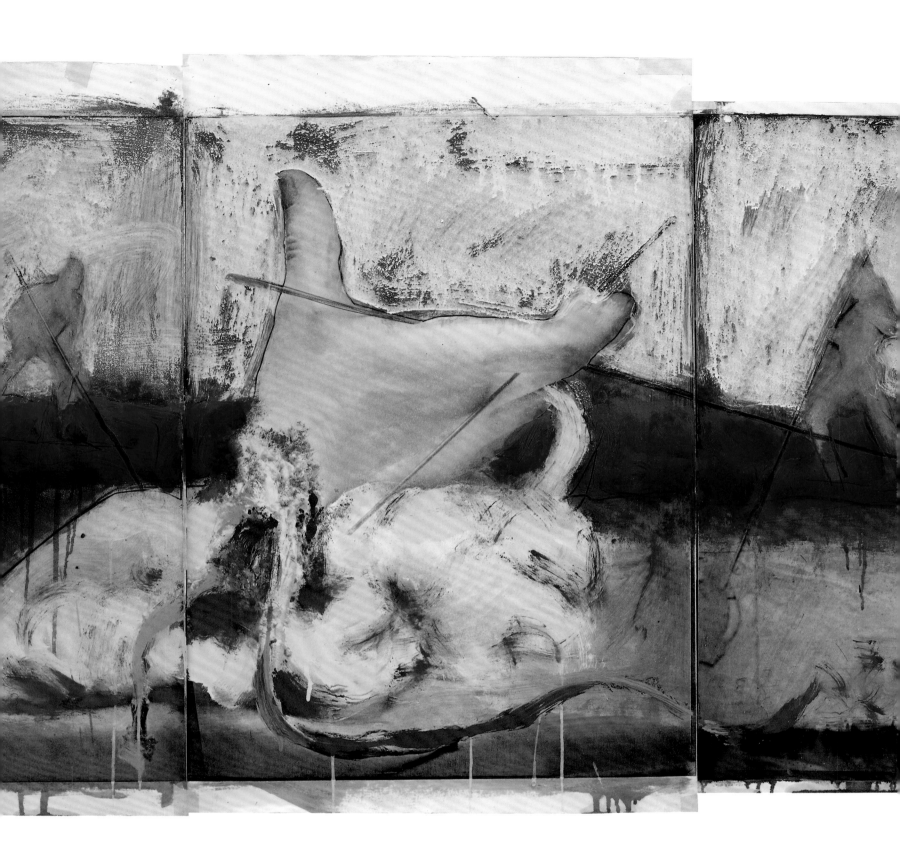

64

Untitled
gravure mono-prints
1992–93

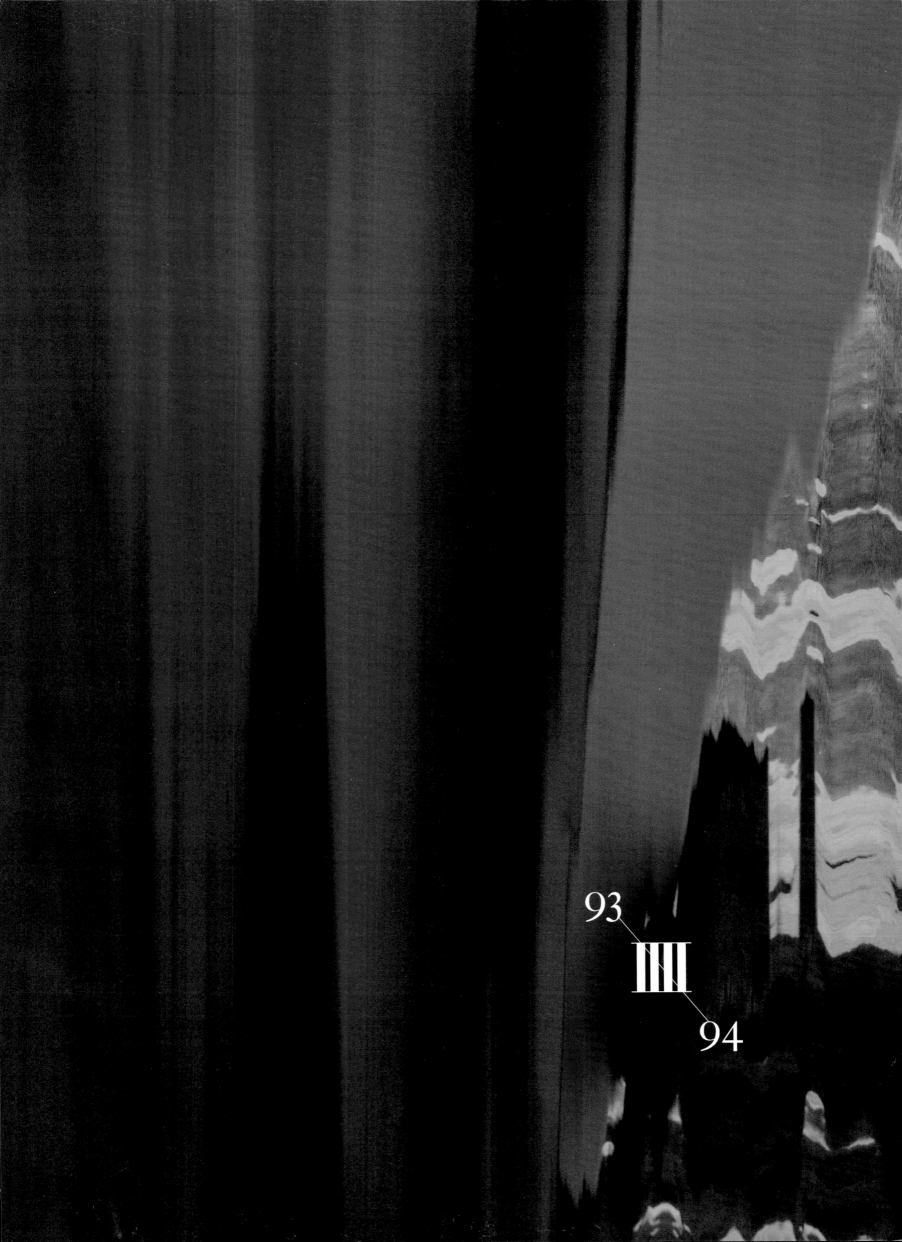

THE EMOTIONAL MORPHOLOGY OF PROCESSING FILM   CHRIS TITTERINGTON

"We none of us enough appreciate the nobleness and sacredness of colour. Nothing is more common than to hear it spoken of as a subordinate beauty – nay, even as the mere source of sensual pleasure... But it is not so. Such expressions are used for the most part in thoughtless-ness; and if the speakers would only take the pains to imagine what the world would become, if the blue were taken from the sky, and the gold from the sunshine, and the verdure from the leaves, and the crimson from the blood which is the life of man... if they could but see for an instant, white human creatures living in a white world, – they would soon feel what they owe to colour. The fact is, that, of all God's gifts to the sight of man, colour is the holiest, the most divine, the most solemn. We speak rashly of gay colour and sad colour... All good colour is in some degree pensive, [and] the loveliest is melancholy." JOHN RUSKIN THE STONES OF VENICE (1853) VOL II, CH. V.

There is a certain solemnity in the beauty of these new works by David Hiscock. Visually, they are gorgeous – perhaps even sumptuous, in their likeness to the light and surface of shot silk and taffeta sarsenet; but they appear also to be noble in that special sense meant by Ruskin in the text above. Such beauty is deeply affecting, deeply impressive. In this they share the visual qualities of the colour work by the contemporary painters Gerhard Richter, and even more so, the Irishman Nicholas May.

Along with these sensual depths, however, there is also a solemn beauty in the method by which they are made – though the gravity that one assigns to their making may in fact be learnt by the reflected beauty of the final product. Once the images have been experi-enced it is impossible to tell. Hiscock uses a camera in which film moves past a slit aperture. Like a procession, moving at a stately speed, the film *processes* before the source of the image. The duration of time this takes may be up to three minutes and the artist can thus introduce or remove objects from the field of view at any time during the exposure. An object might record as a drawn out shape for some seconds or minutes before its 'life' is ended as it is removed from the composition. This is most obviously visible in the works in which rectangles of colour appear [page 74 VI]. This idea of the life of the forms is crucial, for it introduces a sense of the sacredness of the action of composition: one decides what one must do, effects it: the film moves on... whatever is done is done. Thus the choice of objects – almost of 'characters' – and the duration of their parts is rendered deliberate and filled with high import. The photograph becomes a stage which records events over time, an arena in which things from the world come into being, or, as it were, surface from their unrecorded state into vis-iblity, before submerging again into their former invisible state; perhaps, like souls, to be reincarnated in a later work. This, or most of this, is true about all acts of representation. Hiscock's achievement here is to have pro-duced work which in its beauty and gravity provokes such meditation on the symbolic or metaphoric activity that he has invested in the work.

Once it is known that the subject of each of these works is the artist himself, that they are self portraits, and that the camera points at his face and torso, then the metaphors of an individual life begin to seem central to the work. It then appears certain that what is being alluded to here is an internal self portrait, and that

Chris Titterington is Assistant Curator of Photographs at the Victoria and Albert Museum, London

Hiscock has resorted to abstraction in an effort to circumvent the problem of representing the mental, or immaterial interior, by the use of 'exterior' objects. It is indeed difficult for us today to 'read' the personifications of Renaissance art in that way that it was intended, and it takes an effort of mind to understand that William Blake's figures frequently represent psychological 'personalities' and qualities; that they are visual embodiments – vehicles – for a portrait of his own mind. These new works by David Hiscock thus take their place amongst the abstract paintings of Hilma Af Klint and Annie Besant and Charles Leadbeater's 'Thought Forms'. Their internal organization thus comes to stand for patterns of feeling and contesting ideas; for the complexity of the meaning and emotion implicit in the subtle electrical structures that we contain – the tiniest voltages of memory and desire. The photographs become the material equivalents of the artist's internal architecture – his emotional morphology – his *human* silhouette.

In a number of these works, two forms, roughly elleptical, stand upright in an indeterminate space [page 70–73]. They seem to be anthropomorphic like two life-forms, their literal human shape shrouded by an aura. Could they indeed be seen as individuals or are they to be read as individual aspects of a single personality? The beauty of the work is such that the works seem to be visually magnetic, to radiate a presence – like an impressive personality which seems to project attraction. But the work is veiled and would seem to conceal the human – hint at its presence – but keep it well hidden, protected like the holy of holies in the First Temple. In other words, at a time when such views are theoretically unfashionable, is this a declaration in a belief in the numinous individuality of the self – a silent pointing akin to that of Hermeticism or the Cabala? The physiognomy is indeed hidden: his eyes and his whole face, both traditionally considered to be windows on the soul, are concealed – but could they be reconstructed? Might not one be able to pull the drawn out strands of the image together, and like Holbein's anamorphic skull in 'The Ambassadors' at the National Gallery, view the images from the correct angle to put the image into the right perspective?

In retrospect it appears that the subject of this new work has always been Hiscock's subject – that he has always alluded to the growth and state of his own mental economy – his moral and intellectual fabric. The early references to alchemy should have been enough of a clue – being seen as a symbol for the refinement of the soul from baser states of being. The Olympic work seems also to have this theme at its core – Hiscock appears to have been alive to the mental qualities required of the competing individuals, the forces that drive them, their idealism. In this he shows similarity to artists such as Matthew Barney, who sees the development of mental power as similar to that of the development of muscle – that is as the action of the psyche against restraining forces.

The quality of mind revealed in these and Hiscock's earlier works is that of an artist who sees the movements of the spirit even in the mundane. The colour produced in the new works is that of the artist's clothing and his face – both concieved of as clothes of another kind. Here I am put in mind of Thomas Carlyle:

"…The thing Visible, nay the thing Imagined, the thing in any way conceived as visible, what is it but a Garment, a clothing of the Invisible, 'unimaginable, formless, dark with excess of bright. […] What is man himself and his whole terrestrial life, but an Emblem; a Clothing or visible Garment for that divine Me of his, cast hither, like a light–particle, down from Heaven?" SARTOR RESARTUS (1833) BK I, CH. XI

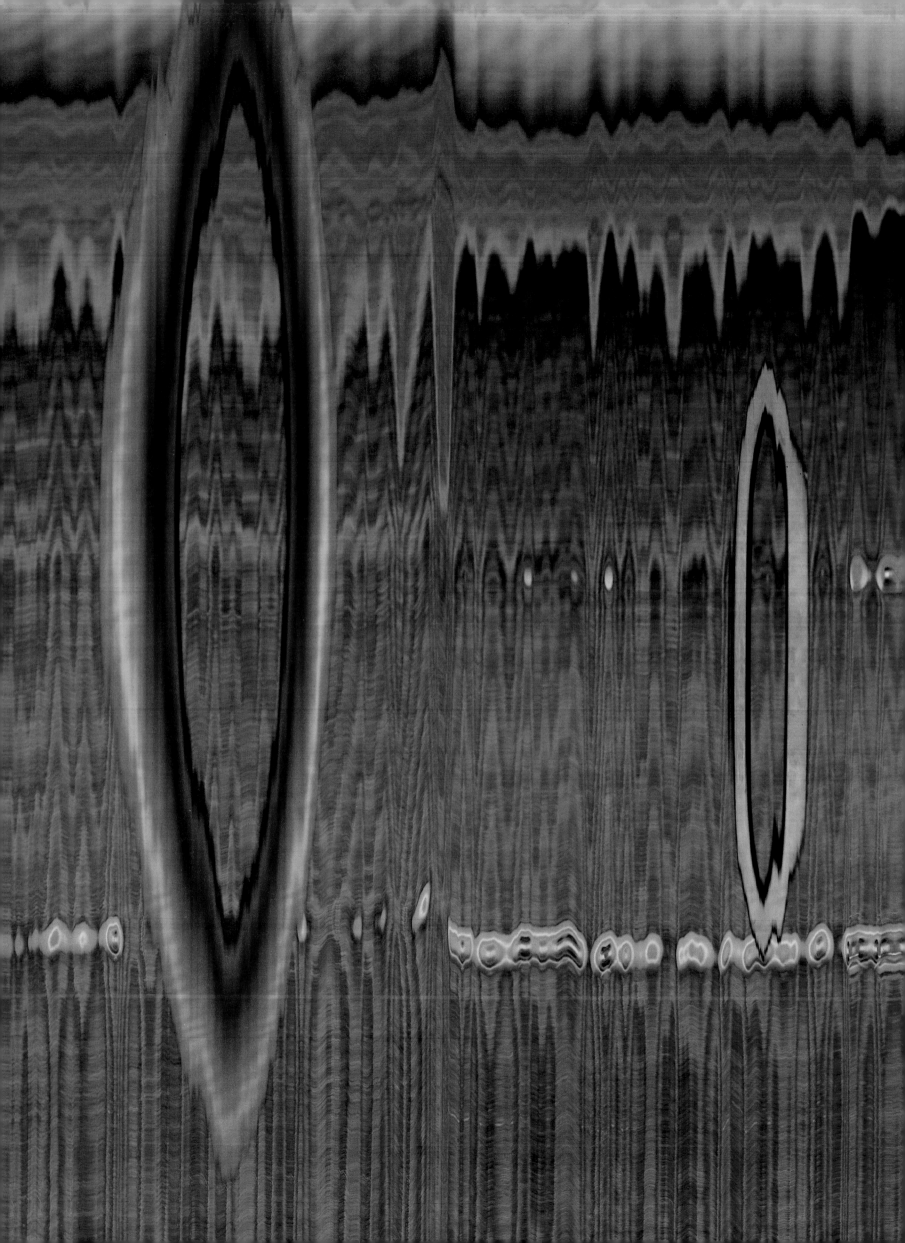

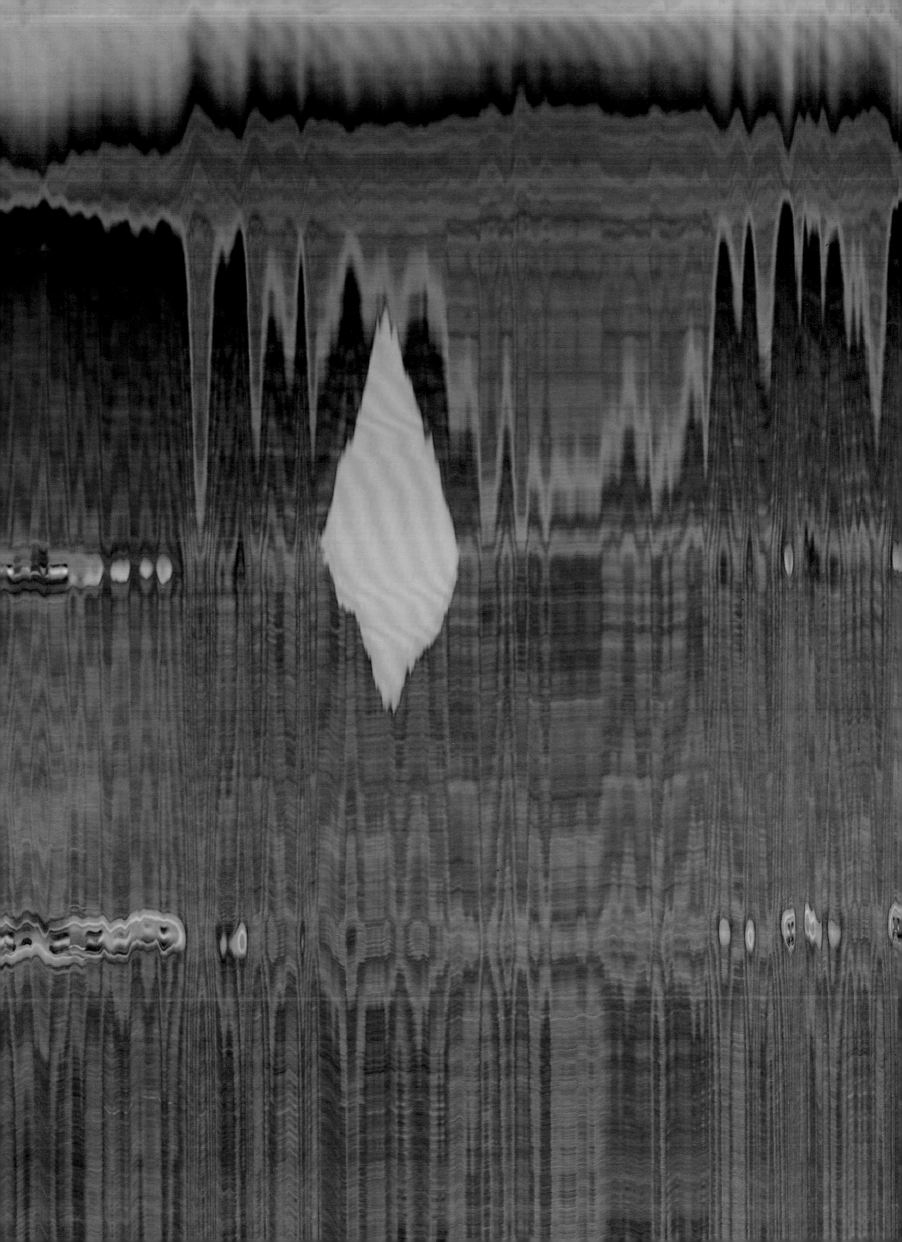

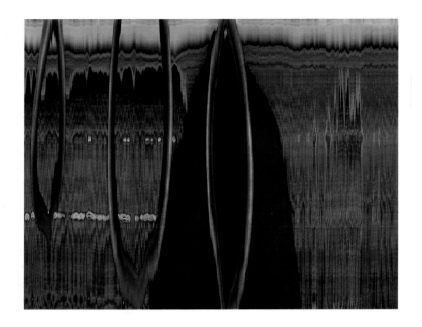

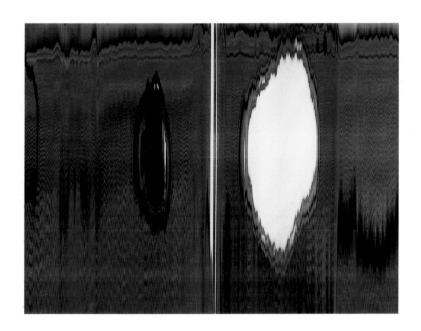

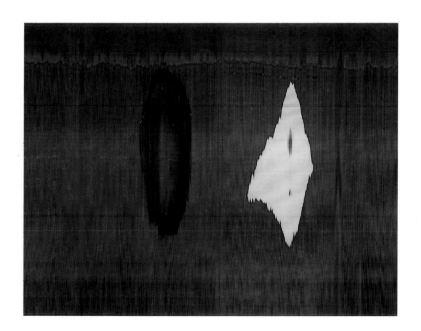

Ouroboros VII   VIII
XI   X
XII   VIII
1993

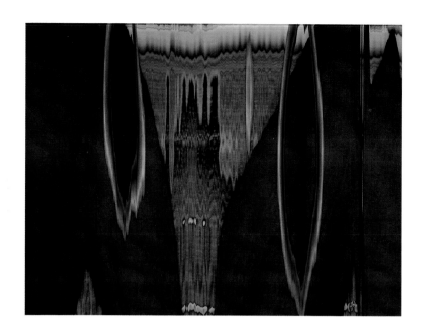

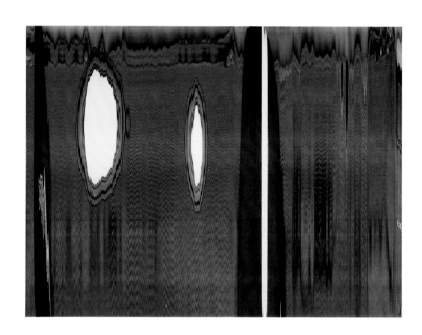

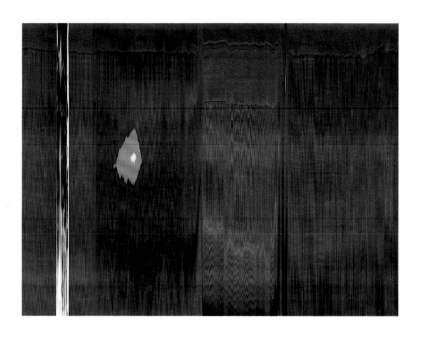

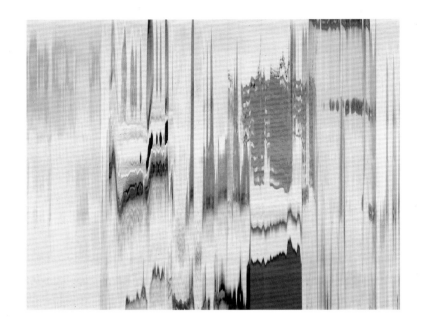

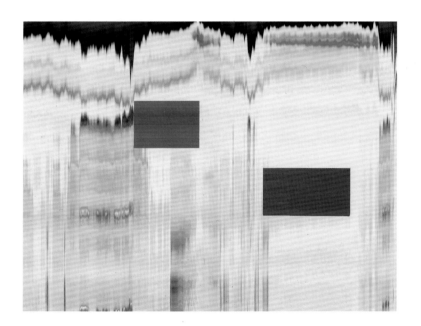

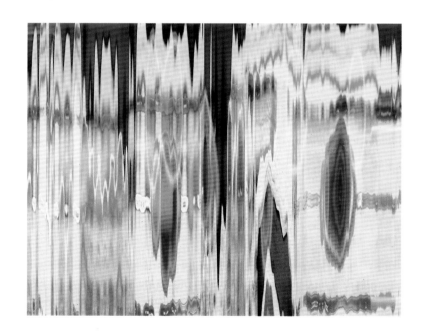

Untitled II   I
        VI III
        IV V
         1993

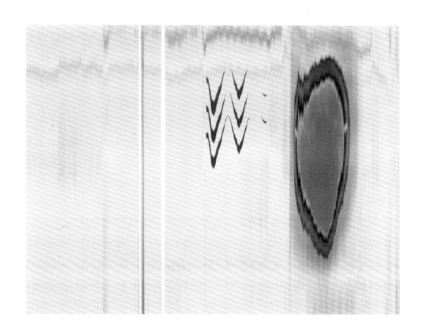

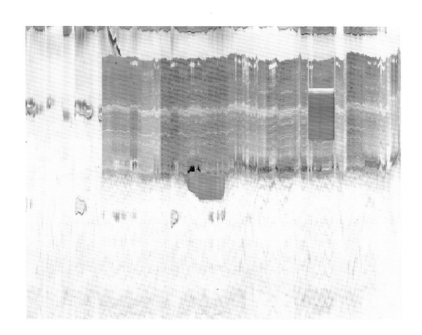

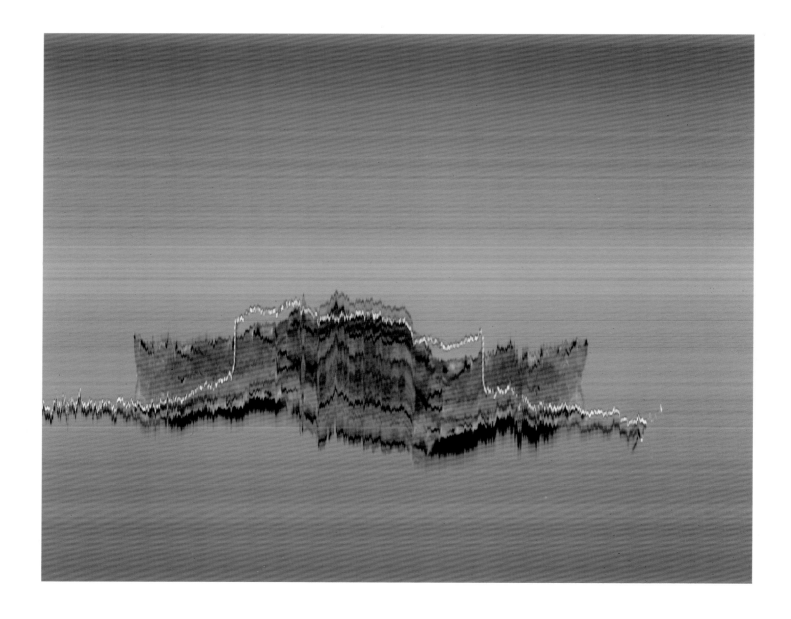

Untitled XXIX
1993

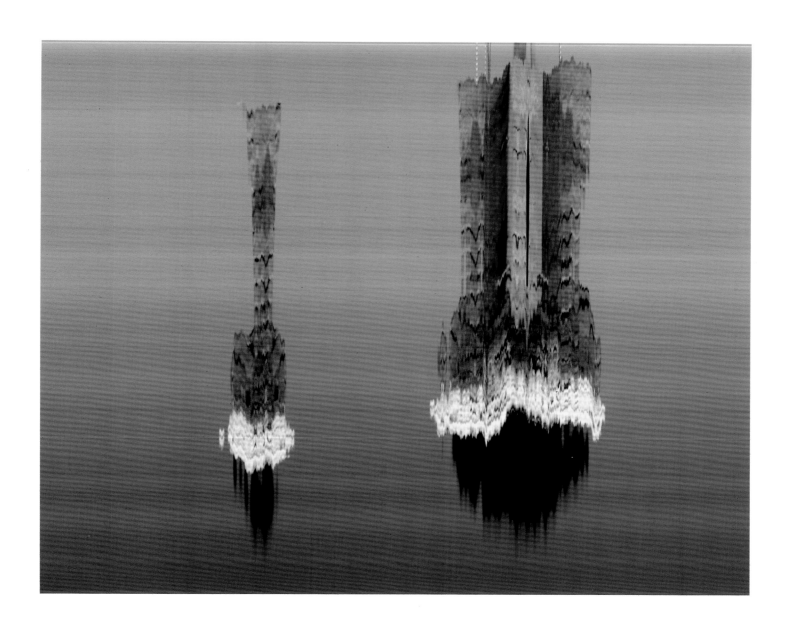

Untitled XXX

1993

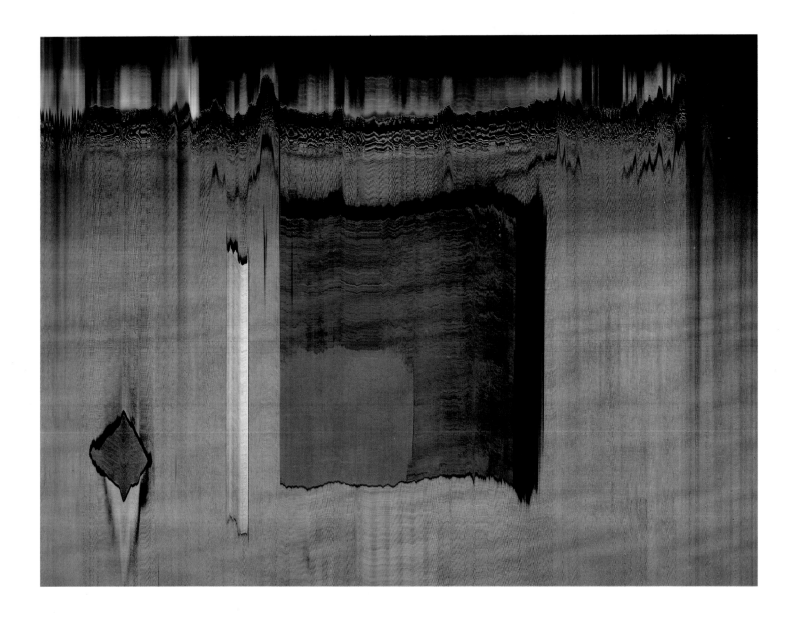

Untitled XXV

1993

Untitled XXVI
1993

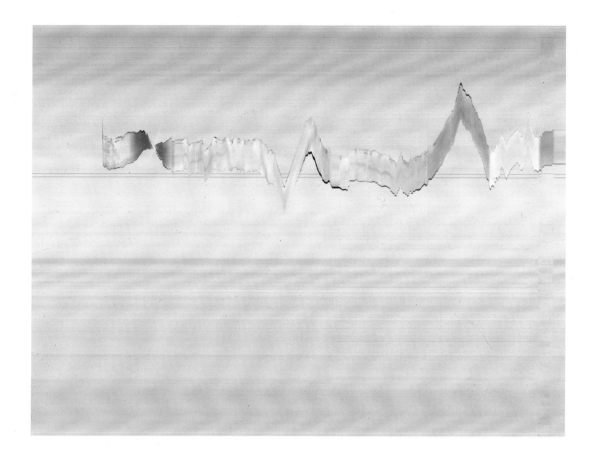

Transmutation XII, XIII & XIV
1993

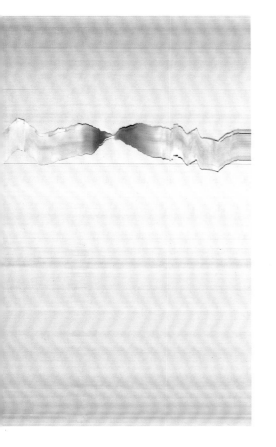
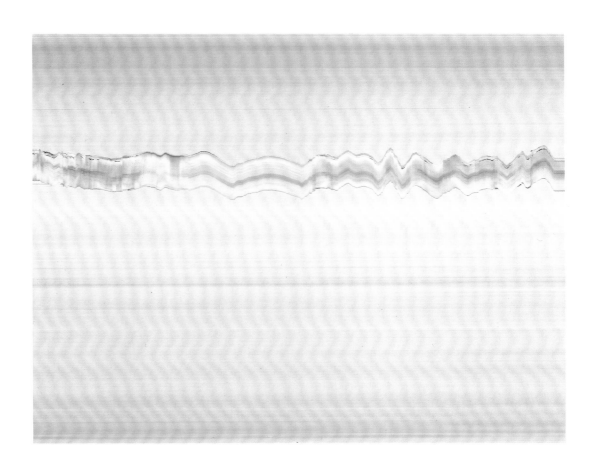

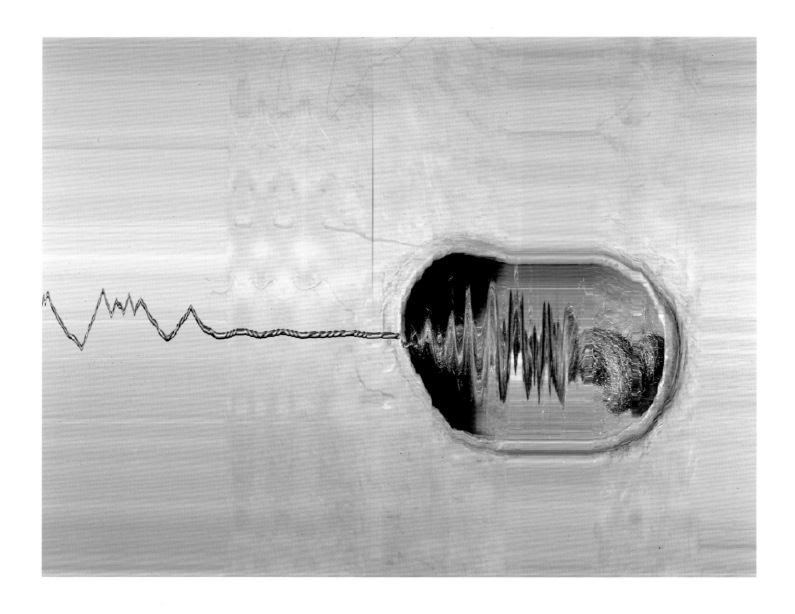

Transmutation VI
1993

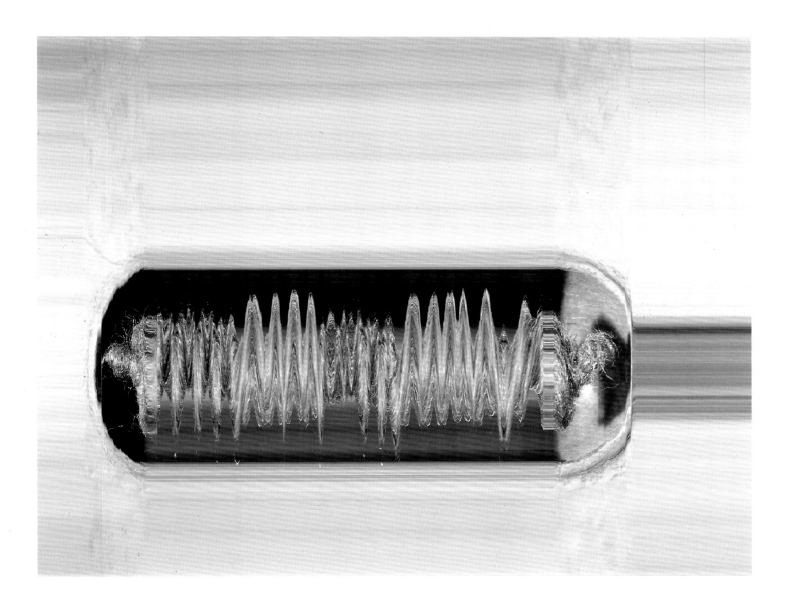

Transmutation IX
1993

Transmutation XV, Clasp

1994

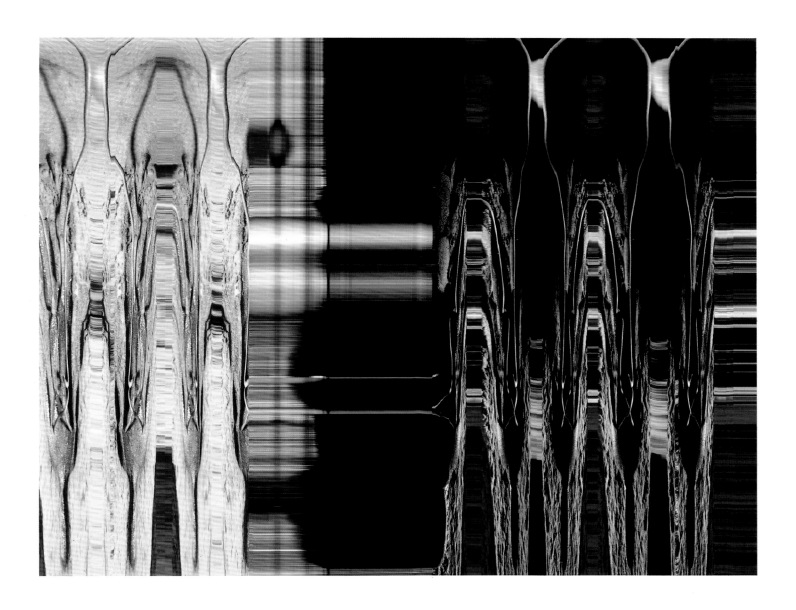

Transmutation XVII, Atlas
1994

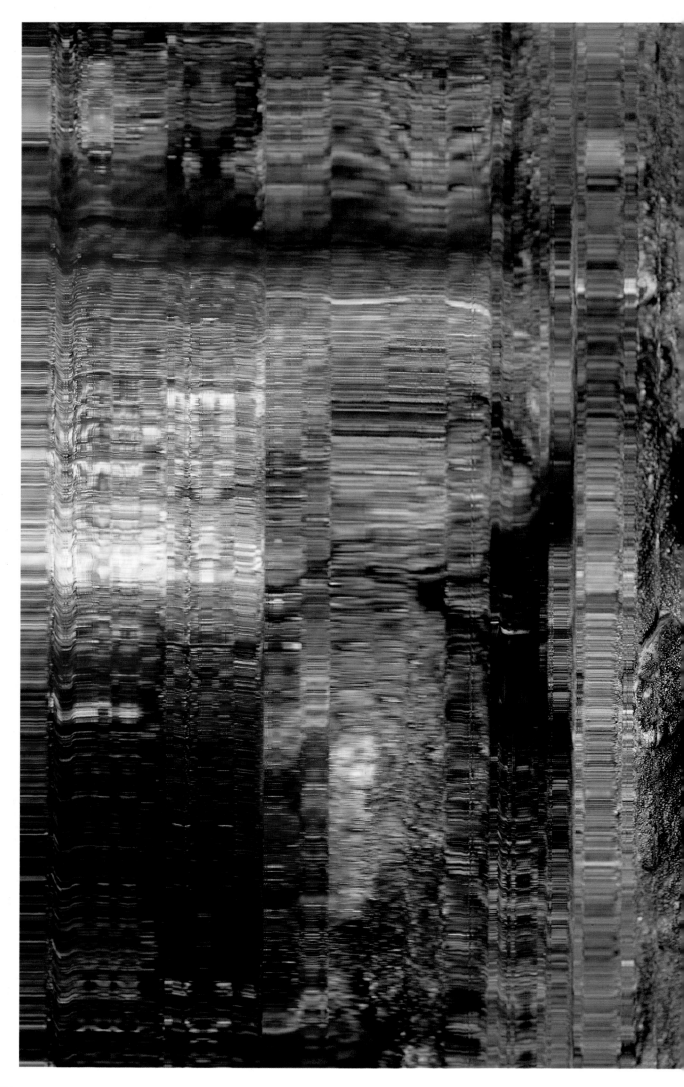

Transmutation XVIV

1994

Transmutation XXII & XXIII, Vessel
1994

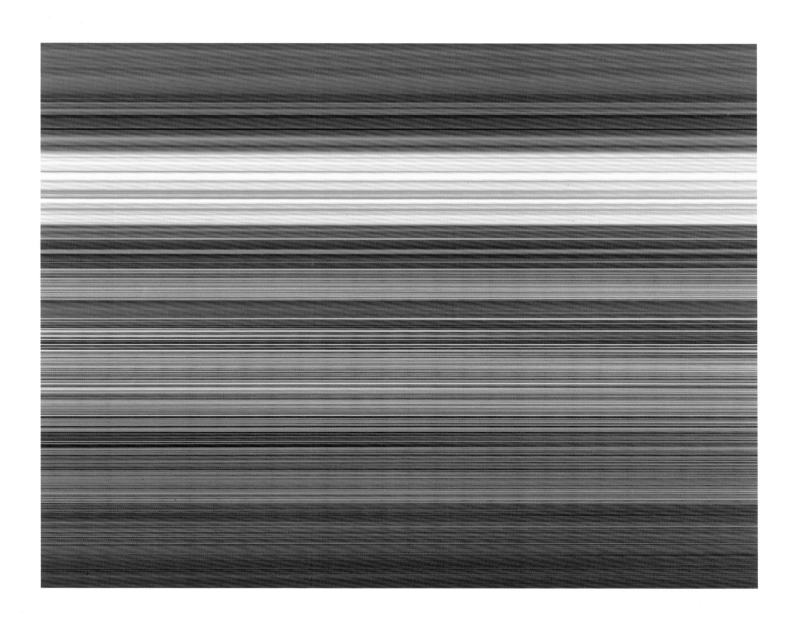

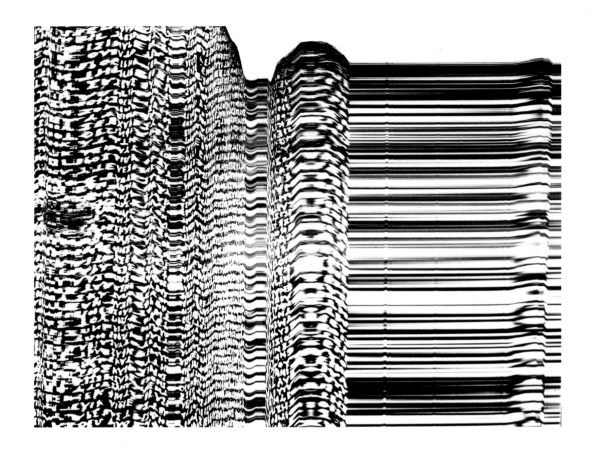

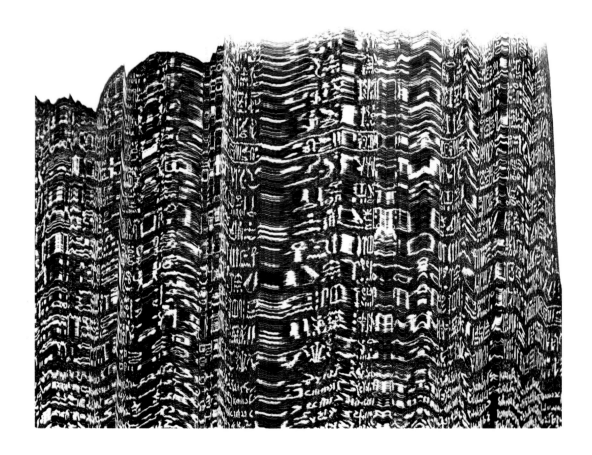

Transmutation, Rosetta Stone
1994

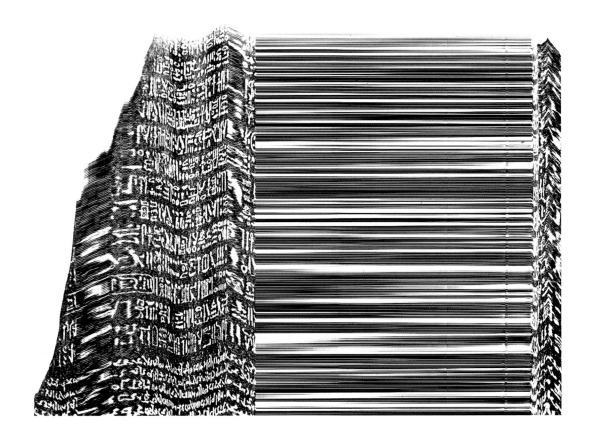

4   IN THE TIME OF THE BLUEBELLS 1987 Photograph and mixed media on panel, 81.5 x 105 cms
Edition of 10 Dye Imbition prints, 20" x 16"

6   SALLY 1994 Photograph and mixed media on card, 12.7 x 10 cms

I

15   HEAD WITH LAURELS 1985 Photogravure, 50 x 52 cms, Edition of 50

16-17   THREE BACKS 1985 Photograph and mixed media on panel, Triptych – each 60 x 78 cm
Edition of 10 Dye Imbition prints, 20" x 16"/ 20" x 24" Dye Imbition prints

18-19   UNTITLED 1985 Unique chlorobromide print, Triptych – each 16" x 12"

20   UNTITLED 1982 Edition of 5 C-type prints, 20" x 24"

21   AARON 1987 Photograph and mixed media on panel, 68.5 x 44 cms
Edition of 10 Dye Imbition prints, 20" x 16"

22 (Top) THREE GRACES 1989 Photograph and mixed media on panel, 233 x 148 cms
Edition of 5 Dye Imbition prints, 20" x 24" / Edition of 5 Dye Imbition prints, 24" x 48"

22   THREE GRACES 1989 Unique Dye Imbition print, 20" x 16"

23   THREE GRACES 1989 (maquette) Photograph and mixed media on card, 23 x 30 cms

25   TOWARDS ACELDAMA 1989 Photograph and mixed media on panel, 245 x 152 x 10 cms

26-27   THE GATES OF HELL 1989-1990 Photograph and mixed media on panel
Diptych – each 152 x 137 x 2 cms, 30" x 40" Dye Imbition print

28-29   SEVEN AGES 1990 Set of 7 photogravures, Edition of 50, 61.5 x 50 cms each

30-31   OMBRA MAI FU 1990 Dye Imbition with mixed media on glass, Triptych – 184 x 100 cms each

32-33   THE FIRE SERMON 1991 Edition of 5 Dye Imbition prints, Diptych - each 30" x 40"

35   THE DEATH OF CLASSICISM 1991 Edition of 5 Dye Imbition prints, 30" x 40"

II

39   HEAD WITH LAURELS 1992 Copper and mixed media on panel, 50 x 52 cms
Edition of 10 Dye Imbition prints, 20" x 24"

40   LONG JUMPERS 1992 Photograph and mixed media on panel, 126.5 x 200.5 cms
Edition of 10 Dye Imbition prints, 20" x 24"

41   LONG JUMPER 1992 Photograph and mixed media on panel, 103.5 x 173 cms
Edition of 10 Dye Imbition prints, 20" x 24"

43   KRIS AKABUSSI 1992 Photograph and mixed media on panel, 112.5 x 146 cms
Edition of 10 Dye Imbition prints, 20" x 24"

44   UNKNOWN SWIMMER 1992 Photograph and mixed media on panel, 80 x 62.5 cms
Edition of 10 Dye Imbition prints, 20" x 24"

45   ADRIAN MOORHOUSE 1992 Edition of 10 Dye Imbition prints, 20" x 24"

46   TRACEY MILES 1992 Numbered chlorobromide prints, 16" x 12"
UNKNOWN SWIMMER Numbered chlorobromide print, 16" x 12"

47   TRACEY MILES 1992 Photograph and mixed media on panel, 100.5 x 75 cms
Edition of 10 Dye Imbition prints, 20" x 24"

49   TWO WRESTLERS 1992 Photograph and mixed media on panel, 49 x 59 cms
Edition of 10 Dye Imbition prints, 20" x 24"

50-51   DUNCAN GOODHEW 1992 Photograph and mixed media, 49 x 104 cms
Numbered chlorobromide prints, 16" x 12"

52-53   EQUIPMENT STILL-LIFE SERIES 1992 Photograph and graphite on card, 2.5" x 3.5"
Numbered C-type prints, 5" x 4"

55   GRAVITATION I 1992 Photogravure, copper and stone on panel, 106.5 x 36 x 10 cms
GRAVITATION II 1992 Photogravure, copper and steel on panel, 106.5 x 36 x 10 cms

57   ANAMNESIS 1992 Photograph, mixed media and metal on panel, 69 x 97 cms
Edition of 10 Dye Imbition prints, 20" x 24"

III

IIII

BIOGRAPHICAL DETAILS

Born: 20 September 1956, England. Education: 1975-1976 Salisbury School of Art / 1976-1979 St. Martins College of Art, London, BA (Hons) Fine Art / 1983-1985 The Royal College of Art, MA Photography

SOLO EXHIBITIONS

1987 The Royal Photographic Society, Bath / 1988 Pomeroy Purdy Gallery, London
1989 The Photographer's Gallery, London / 1990 Parco Gallery, Tokyo, Japan. Toured Osaka, Nagoya, Sapporo
Pomeroy Purdy Gallery, London / The Norwich Art Centre, Norwich
1991 Galerie du Chateau d'Eau, Toulouse, France / Galerie Espace St. Cyprien, Toulouse, France
1992 Pomeroy Purdy Gallery, London / Zelda Cheatle Gallery, London / The Castlefields Gallery, Manchester
Toured Edinburgh, Norwich, Aberdeen / 1993 Zelda Cheatle Gallery, London
1994 'Transmutations', Purdy Hicks Gallery, London

SELECTED GROUP SHOWS

1985 'Prelude', Kettle's Yard, Cambridge / 'La Creative Britannique', Printemps, Paris
1986 'A Show of Hands', Sheffield City Art Gallery / The Royal Photographic Society, Bath
International Contemporary Art Fair, London / 'Twenty For Today', National Portrait Gallery, London
'David Hiscock & David Newman', West Oxfordshire Arts Association
1987 '150 Years of The Royal College of Art', Barbican Centre, London / 'Painting/Photography/Painting',
Richard Pomeroy Gallery, London / 'A Private View', The Royal Photographic Society, Bath
1988 'Photography on the Edge', Haggarty Museum, Wisconsin, U.S.A.
'Open Exhibition', The Royal Society of Painters,Etchers & Engravers,The Bankside Gallery, London
'The Art of Lego', Wrexham, Clwyd / 'Object and Image', Stoke on Trent Museum and Art Gallery
'Art Relief Bangladesh', Business Art Galleries, London / 'L.A. Art Fair', Los Angeles, U.S.A.
1989 'Figure II, Naked', Victoria Art Gallery, Bath / 'Fictive Strategies', Squibb Gallery, Princeton,
New Jersey, U.S.A. / 'Blasphemies, Ecstasies, Cries', Serpentine Gallery, London
Toured Norwich School of Art, Mostyn Art Gallery / 'Summer Show', Zelda Cheatle Gallery, London
'21 Years of Photography', The Royal College of Art, London / 'The Annual International Print Exhibition',
The Royal Photographic Society, Bath / 'Machine Dreams', The Photographers' Gallery, London
1990 'Identities', Philadelphia Art Alliance, Philadelphia, U.S.A. / 'Rencontres Photographiques',
Carcassone, France / 'Face On', Zelda Cheatle Gallery, London / 'David Hiscock & Calum Colvin',
The Seagate Gallery, Dundee / 'Gallery Artists', Pomeroy Purdy Gallery, London
1991 'David Hiscock & Calum Colvin', Oriel Gallery, Cardiff. Toured Theatre Clwyd, Mold
'Art Now', Beak Street Gallery, London
1992 'Works by 54 Master Printers', John Jones Gallery, London / 'The Figure Laid Bare', Pomeroy
Purdy Gallery, London / 'Print Centre Editions', Pomeroy Purdy Gallery, London
'Visa Olympic Art '92', Palais Moya, Barcelona
1993 AIPAD Art Fair, New York / 'Gallery Artists', Purdy Hicks Gallery, London / Cologne Art Fair, Cologne
The Freshfields Gallery, Freshfields, London / 'Fictions of the Self', Weatherspoon Art Gallery, University
of North Carolina / Toured Herter Art Gallery, University of Massachusetts / Palazzio del Exhibition, Rome
Museum of Modern Art, Nice / 'New Work', Zelda Cheatle Gallery, London
1994 'Drawing', Purdy Hicks Gallery, London / 'The Journey', Gallery K, London
'Time Machine', British Museum, London
1995 'A Positive View', Saatchi Gallery, London

AWARDS

1983-1985 Pentax Bursary
1984-1985 Vogue Award for Photography
1985 Madame Tussaud's Award for Figurative Work
1987 The Photographer's Gallery Trust Fund (Runner-up for Portraiture)
The Ilford Photographic Awards (First Prize and Highly Commended, Advertising/Fashion Category)
1989 The Royal Photographic Society (Print Competition Winner)
1992 The Official British Olympic Artist (Sponsored by Visa, Barcelona Olympic Games)
The Ilford Photographic Awards (First Prize and Highly Commended, Advertising/Fashion Category)

COLLECTIONS

National Portrait Gallery, London / The Royal Photographic Society, Bath / Haggerty Museum, Wisconsin
Visa International, London & Olympic Museum, Lausanne / L' Espace Saint Cyprien, Toulouse
Gallerie du Chateau d'Eau, Toulouse / Madame Tussaud's

SELECTED BIBLIOGRAPHY

'La Creative Britannique' Royal College of Art & Printemps Haussmann, 1985 (Cat.)

'Twenty For Today - New Portrait Photography', Pepper, T. National Portrait Gallery, 1986 (Cat.)

'Exposure - Photographs from Blitz Magazine, 1980 - 1987', Ebury Press, 1987

'Portrait of an Artist', Biddulph, F. Traditional Interior Decoration, June/July 1988

'David Hiscock', Laroche, J. Zoom, no. 41, 1988

'Machine Dreams', Chandler, D. The Photographer's Gallery, 1989 (Cat.)

'Photographers at The Royal College of Art', Royal College of Art, 1989 (Cat.)

'One Hundred and Thirty Third Annual International Print Exhibition', The Royal Photographic Society, 1989 (Cat.)

'Identities - Portraiture in Contemporary Photography', Hay Halpert, P. (ed.) Philadelphia Art Alliance, 1990 (Cat.)

'Styling Front - Photo', Styling Magazine – Tokyo, June 1990

'David Hiscock - In Conversation', Pomeroy Purdy Gallery, 1990

'David Hiscock', Juncosa, E. Pomeroy Purdy Gallery, 1990 (Cat.)

'David Hiscock', Hodgson, F. Skoob Books, 1990

'La Galerie du Chateau d'Eau presente David Hiscock', Vis a Vis International, No. 9, 1991

'The Art of Going for Gold', Tyrrel, R. The Mail on Sunday, 19 January 1992

'A Moving Picture Show', Palmer, A. The Independent, March 1992

'Photo Finish for a Load of Old Junk', Boggan, S. The Independent, March 1992

'Visa Olympic Art 1992', Visa international Service association, 1992 (Cat.)

'Photographic Finish for a Pools Winner', The Sunday Times Magazine, 3 May 1992

'Games Without Rules', McCabe, E. The Guardian, 24 May 1992

'This Sporting Life', McSweeney, E. Vogue Magazine, June 1992

'Olympic Images', Esquire Magazine, June 1992

'Photo-Finish', Linklater, A. The Telegraph Magazine, 6 June 1992

'Off the Beaten Track', British Journal of Photography, 18 June 1992

'Olympic Images', Creative Review, June 1992

'Special Olympic Visa Art supplement', Ellison, H. The International Herald Tribune, July 1992

'Winner Takes Bronze', Alberge, D. The Independent, 7 July 1992

'David Hiscock at Zelda Cheatle', Cooper, E. Time Out Magazine, 15-22 July 1992

'Message and Image', Juncosa, E. Portfolio Magazine, Summer 1992

'David Hiscock', Heuser, M. Zoom Magazine, No. 121, February 1993

'David Hiscock', Creative Review, January 1994

'David Hiscock', Time Out, 4-11 May 1994

'That Unfathomable Thing, David Hiscock's Transmuation: Rosetta Stone', Mellor, D.A., Portfolio, Number 20, 1994

Published 1995 by zelda cheatle press, 8 Cecil Court , London WC2N 4HE, Tel 0171 836 0506, Fax 0171 497 8911
All images reproduced in this book are available as original signed prints from the zelda cheatle gallery.

© zelda cheatle press Ltd. All photographs © David Hiscock. Text © Dr David Mellor and Christopher Titterington
Edited by Michael Mack. Designed by Howard Brown. Printed by Balding & Mansell.

ISBN 0 9518371 9 2

British Library Cataloguing in Publication Data. A catalogue record for this book is available from the British Library.